ALEC CLIFTON-TAYLOR

TOTNES

C000125561

BRITISH BROADCASTING CORPORATION

The photographs in this book, apart from those listed below, were taken by Geoff Howard and reproduced from prints made by Michael Spry of Downtown Darkroom.

Acknowledgement is due to the following for permission to reproduce illustrations (the figures refer to plate numbers): Aerofilms, front cover; National Monuments Record 2, 3 (copyright B. T. Batsford); *Torquay Herald Express*, 23.

The plan was drawn by ESR Ltd, cartographers.

Published by the
British Broadcasting Corporation
35 Marylebone High Street
London W1M 4AA

First published 1978 as a chapter in *Six English Towns*
This edition first published 1984
© Alec Clifton-Taylor 1978

ISBN 0 563 20290 4

Printed in England by
Jolly & Barber Ltd,
Rugby, Warwickshire

TOTNES

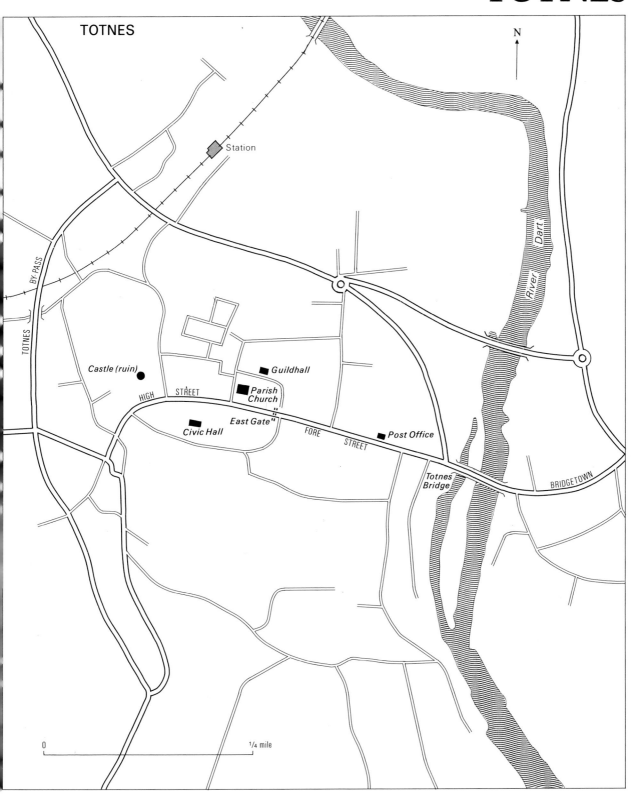

TOTNES

N

Station

River Dart

TOTNES BY-PASS

Castle (ruin)

HIGH STREET

Guildhall

Parish Church

Civic Hall

East Gate

FORE STREET

Post Office

Totnes Bridge

BRIDGETOWN

0   ¼ mile

1. *Totnes – town plan*

2. *East Gate from Fore Street in 1944*

Near the end of the eighth century King Alfred established in Devon four forts, to counter the menace of the Danes. The chief was Exeter: one of the other *burhs*, as they were called, was Halwell. About 950 this burh was moved five miles farther north, to a much more easily defensible site, which was Totnes.

The name derives from two Saxon words, *tot*, which means a look-out, and *nais*, or ness, which means literally a nose, and in this case was a nose of land projecting into a valley – the valley of the Dart, which originally lapped three sides of it. For about a hundred years, from 1750 to 1850, the usual spelling was Totness; then for some reason they reverted to the old orthography.

It was an excellent site, the more so as in Saxon times the river was tidal up to this point and, for boats of shallow draught, navigable. Here the Dart could be forded. And there is still no bridge across it seaward of Totnes. Under Edgar (958–975) the place had its own mint.

In the spring of 1069 William the Conqueror laid siege to Exeter. Before long the whole of the South-West thence to Land's End capitulated without a fight. The lordship of Totnes, and of 107 other manors in Devon, was granted to Judhael, one of William's Breton followers. He erected, at the highest point of the town, a castle of earth and timber: the earthworks were on a big scale. In 1088 he also founded a Priory, as a cell of Angers, which survived until the Dissolution.

A century later the circular keep, which is seventy feet in diameter, was rebuilt in stone, the very coarse stone of this locality. Long ago this region was volcanic, and layers of volcanic ash, deposited in water, ultimately became cemented into solid rocks. That is what this stone is: volcanic ash or tuff. Together with a certain amount of dolerite or 'greenstone', another igneous rock found in association with the tuffs, this is the principal building stone of Totnes. It was quarried on the southern outskirts of the town and just across the river.

There is nothing to see now inside, but the shell of the keep, which was strengthened in 1326, has been carefully restored. Since 1485 it has been used neither as a fortress nor as a residence, but, oddly enough, this Castle, with a bailey on the steep side facing away from the town, has always remained in private ownership. In 1559 it was acquired by the Seymours, and in 1947 the Duke of Somerset transferred it to the care of what was then the Ministry of Works, now the Department of the Environment. Perhaps the principal reason for climbing up the motte today is to enjoy the views from the ramparts.

Totnes acquired walls, but only short sections were ever of stone, as after the Conquest fortifications were not needed here. The rest were merely earth ramparts and fences, or in places just a stout timber palisade. Although it was reconstructed in 1835 with a wider opening, much the best relic of the ancient circuit of walls is the East Gate, half-way up the hill (2, 3).

*3. East Gate
from High Street
in 1929*

At the time of Domesday (1086) there were ninety-five houses within the walls and fifteen more outside. By then there was already a wooden bridge over the Dart, which gave place about 1210 to a new one in stone. The bridge, which was less than five feet wide and had eight arches, not all alike, was maintained by a chantry foundation until 1548. Then the Corporation took it over. But even after 1692, when its width was doubled, heavy carts still had to use the fords. The present bridge, of three arches, a fine one in grey Devonian limestone (5) by the Devon-born architect Charles Fowler, was opened in 1828, the year in which he designed his most famous work, Covent Garden Market. Until 1882 a toll had to be paid to cross it.

Prosperity, as usual, depended on trade. Totnes has always been the market town for a rich agricultural district. In the eighteenth century, when half the male population was engaged in farming, that was its chief function. But earlier, various other trades had flourished. One of the first, dating back at least to the twelfth century, was tanning. Percy Russell, the historian of Totnes, recorded that in 1244 the lord of the manor

6

allowed the Abbot of Torre to purchase sixty hides a year free of toll, in return for two pairs of boots at Michaelmas. Another early industry was slate-quarrying. As long ago as 1180, 800,000 of the local slates were shipped to Winchester, for its Castle. The trade in woollen cloth became important in the thirteenth century, and so did ironwork from the local smithies. There was some ship-building too, and a flourishing trade in meat and fish: under Elizabeth I quantities of pilchards were landed here to be salted and packed into barrels. But as a port Totnes fought a losing battle against Dartmouth. The Dart had to be dredged continually. When, about 1580, Dartmouth embarked upon a highly successful trade in cod, Totnes had no share in it.

Fifty years earlier, principally because of its export trade, Totnes is said to have become the richest town in Devon after Exeter. And the fifteenth century, also a good period, had seen the rebuilding of the Church. The castle has the loftier site, but it is the imposing tower of the church (7) that is the focal point of many a distant view (4). To raise it must have been a formidable undertaking for a town with a population which until a hundred years ago was always well under 4000. It was really due to the energy and enthusiasm of three successive mayors, who, we read, 'drove the townsmen hard'. Some were ordered to go and work in the quarry, which was probably over the hills some miles to the east, near Paignton. For the stone of the tower is not the local tuff but a deep red Permian sandstone, which was brought in barges round the Brixham peninsula and

6 *(far left).*
Ashburton
church tower

7 *(left).*
Totnes
church tower

up the Dart to a new quay close to the bridge specially built for it. From there it was dragged up the hill by horses, or perhaps oxen.

We know that in 1450 the overseers had to go and look at four other church towers and to make Totnes 'according to the best model among them', a very typical way of proceeding in the Middle Ages. The tower was evidently a great status symbol. One of the towers specified was Ashburton (6), which has much smaller pinnacles but is otherwise similar in design, although differing in colour and texture because this one is of grey Devonian limestone. Both are striking examples of the Devon type of tower, which hardly occurs outside this county, apart from three in West Somerset. The great feature is the stair turret, often projecting from the middle of one side, usually the south, but at Ashburton the north side. These bold towers with their sweeping lines, strong silhouettes, very small windows and general absence of ornamentation hold a great fascination for some modern architects.

The rest of the church is a mixture of stones, with dark-toned tuffs predominating (8). The red sandstone was used mainly for dressings and for the porch. The gable of the latter and the south aisle parapet, added early in the seventeenth century, are of whitish

8

limestone from Beer in East Devon, which has not worn very well. The Devonian limestone used in the nineteenth century for an additional north aisle is considerably tougher.

With its mainly indifferent pews, hard shiny tiles and poor glass, the interior of this church is no longer very enjoyable. But the screen is still very impressive, and unusual in that it is of stone (also from Beer). When it had its images – in the central part three

8. The Church from the south-east

tiers of small statues under canopies – it must have been wonderful. The loft has gone, but the small coved top which has replaced it provides some compensation for its loss. Parts of the screen have been discreetly recoloured.

Cheek by jowl with the Church, on part of the site of the former Priory, stands the Guildhall (9), a modest little edifice dating from 1553. In the octagonal piers of the arcade we have another local building stone: Dartmoor granite. But there is not much granite in Totnes, for they had so much else, even closer to hand.

Within, there is the Court Room, with the town's coat of arms: a gatehouse crowned by three towers, and flanked by a pair of big keys. Visible under the archway of the gate is a raised portcullis, while in front there is water. Whether this was correct was for long uncertain, but a base *water barry wavy*, as the heralds put it, is now the accepted form. And the river Dart was indeed vital to the prosperity of Totnes. Beyond, in the Council Chamber, the arms occur again, twice in fact, the larger being set between the emblems of Justice and Equity (11). Above runs rather a jolly plaster frieze, with a repeating pattern of prancing winged horses, typically Jacobean (10).

The list of Mayors of the Borough of Totnes – over six hundred of them – goes back to 1359. But alas, Totnes, like so many of our smaller historic towns, is no longer a borough: it is now only a parish council. It was one of the many victims of the reorganisation of local government in 1974. What a wretched piece of legislation that was! It distorted time-honoured boundaries, ignored history, invented new counties – grotesque creations like Avon and Humberside – and played havoc with civic powers

9. *The Guildhall*

and pride. In my work I disregard it. Bath for me is still in Somerset, Beverley and Hull
in the East Riding of Yorkshire. Fortunately Devon was left intact.

Totnes does not now have any houses earlier than the sixteenth century, but quite a
number of those in the High Street are of Tudor origin. The main block was usually two
rooms thick and three storeys high, the ground floor being set aside for trade.

12.
*70 Fore Street:
the Museum*

Underneath one side of the first-floor room a passage ran back into a small courtyard, with a second block beyond, containing the kitchen. Behind this was a long strip of land used for stores and workshops, and also, when there was a back entrance, for stables and pigsties. Where this survives it is now usually a garden. The most complete example is 70 Fore St, a merchant's house of about 1575, which in 1971 was turned into a local museum (12).

Now, although usually no longer very apparent, the fronts of all these Tudor houses, and a good many later ones in the older part of Totnes, are still what they always were: timber-framed. In the course of time the wooden frames with their lath and plaster infilling became masked, sometimes under stucco but often under overcoats of slates, hung upon battens across the front of house after house. The side walls were of the coarse local tuff referred to earlier. But the hung slates on the fronts are the special feature of this town's domestic architecture.

These too were quarried locally: so here is yet one more kind of stone which was at the disposal of the builders of Totnes, and a stone of which they availed themselves unstintingly. The rock is Middle Devonian slate of excellent quality, which splits easily to yield thin slabs suitable not only for hanging vertically but also, of course, for roofing: virtually the whole town is roofed with slate (14).

The quarries, although now much overgrown, can still be identified some three or four miles away to the south-west. A former quarrymen's hut in one of them, now in

13.
53–57 Fore Street

ruins, shows that this stone can also be used in more massive blocks for building purposes. Given the right conditions this beautiful slate could of course still be worked today, but none of these quarries has in fact supplied Totnes with slate since about the beginning of the present century. If slates are needed here now, they have to be obtained from Delabole, near Camelford in Cornwall. This was the source of the hung slates used in 1927 for a new Post Office, specially designed to fit in with the town – a

14. *Totnes from the castle*

great credit to the GPO and an ornament to Totnes (16). Would that there were more contemporary architects willing sometimes to sink their own impulse to design something which must at all costs look different, and to recognise that there are some situations where the assertion of too much individuality is just bad manners.

Most of the hung slates in Totnes are merely plain rectangles of varying size (13), but occasionally they cut their slates into fanciful shapes – spoiling a good many in the process, no doubt – and hung them to make decorative patterns (15). These fish-scale-shaped slates are very enjoyable, but at the same time it has to be admitted that decorative slatework is far more resourceful in both France and Germany than it is here. In France fish-scale slates on the *tourelles* of *châteaux* are frequently seen, and never fail to give pleasure. But for slate-hanging at its most brilliant one must go to Hesse, and the little towns fringing the Harz Mountains. A visit to a town such as Goslar leaves one wondering whether our own craftsmen in slate have been sufficiently enterprising.

Totnes has a number of examples of polychrome slate-hanging. Generally slates of contrasting colours were hung in simple horizontal bands, but on the new Civic Hall they are arranged to make large diamonds. A good many people here paint their slates (examples are 95–97 (17) and 105 High Street), and this certainly gives the town a more lively appearance. But I am slightly shocked as a rule by the idea of painting stone; some of the slates at Totnes are certainly too good to be hidden under paint.

Some of these timber-framed – and here also slate-hung – houses still retain oak panelling and, especially, plasterwork dating from the Elizabethan and early Stuart

Opposite:
15 *(top left).*
88 High Street

16 *(top right).*
The Post Office,
Fore Street

17 *(right).*
95–97
High Street

18 *(far left).*
10 High Street

19 *(left).*
32 High Street

periods. At 32 High Street, where there is also a granite chimney piece (19), which is unusual in this town, the panelling dates from 1577, and there is a ribbed plaster ceiling, with parts of a small frieze too. Other late sixteenth-century ceilings are in the first-floor rooms of No. 10 and 16, a little way lower down the street. The ribs of the Elizabethan ceiling were usually narrow. Under her successor they gradually grew broader. At No. 10 the thin ribs enclose Tudor roses and *fleurs de lis* (18). For motifs like these they would certainly have used moulds. Ribbed ceilings were something of a Devon speciality at this time, and can often be found in quite modest houses. Whether Totnes had its own plasterers is not known, but their chief centres in Devon were at Exeter and Barnstaple.

Jacobean plaster ceilings can be seen at 48 and 64 Fore Street, again in upstairs rooms. The former is mainly floral; the latter, dated 1625, is the finest surviving example in the town (20). The ribs have now become flat bands, and their surfaces are enriched with a tightly-knit running ornament of flowers, fruit, foliage and strapwork. The effect is quite sumptuous. Other motifs include jesters, shells, sprays of oak leaves and pine cones, for all of which they made moulds; for this ceiling they must have had at least twenty different ones. But in two lozenges the relief is bolder, and evidently modelled by hand. One has the Prince of Wales's feathers and the initials CP, so it was done just before Charles I succeeded. In the second lozenge is another representation of the town's coat of arms.

20 *(opposite).*
64 Fore Street

But during the seventeenth century Totnes lost some of its former prosperity, and indeed by 1719 the borough was actually insolvent. A year or two after this Defoe was to declare that, although a good town, it contained more gentlemen than traders. Half the men were now farmers or employed by farmers, and the town was the market for live cattle as well as for their produce. The early eighteenth-century architecture is enjoyable but surprisingly unsophisticated. Nos. 26 and 28 High Street (21), which both date from 1707, provide an amusing contrast. No. 28 (the right-hand one) is decidedly folksy.[1] The other has a poor window in the gable but is the better house. A little farther along the High Street it is not difficult to see that the early Georgian features are only skin-deep, over much earlier timber-framing. Many of the old mullioned casement windows were now replaced by sashes.

The High Street is memorable for its shopping arcades, which used to be known here, a little comically, as the *piazzas*: a misunderstanding of the Italian word for an arcaded square. Today they are called the Butterwalks. There are plenty of these covered walks on the continent: one thinks of Bologna, Padua, Innsbruck and many in France. But, perhaps rather surprisingly in view of our climate, they are not common in England, where only one town has more than Totnes, and that of course is Chester. There the famous Rows run along at first-floor level, and originated, no one knows how, right back in the thirteenth century. Here the earliest appeared in 1584, but in their present form they mostly belong to the eighteenth century. They were achieved by extending the upper floors of existing houses outwards, and supporting their outer corners on piers or pillars, either of wood or granite (22). Though the covered arcade

[1]At the back of this house there was once a small theatre. Hence the three masks on the keystones.

23 *(far left).*
Gothick House,
Bank Lane

24 *(left).*
47 Fore Street

was welcome, house-owners were also glad to make this alteration because they secured more accommodation. They had therefore to pay an annual charge for encroachment. At one time stalls used to be set up under the arcades, but this of course did not suit the shopkeepers, and was presently prohibited.

Most of the architectural interest of this old town is to be found in one long, steep, narrow and, at the top end, winding street (1), which, even though it has been by-passed and is for one-way traffic only, can still become very much congested. One would like to see parts, if not all, of it become a pedestrian precinct, but for the shopkeepers there are some practical difficulties in the way.

The East Gate separates the upper part, High Street, from the lower part, Fore Street. It is rather a pity that it has been covered with stucco (2, 3). A little below it, up a side alley, is a gem of Gothick: the most entertaining house in Totnes, not least because a public footpath passes right through it! (23) (Incidentally, the back is slate-hung and not Gothick at all.)

Brick made a very late appearance in this town: even in the eighteenth century it was only very sparingly employed. There is one enjoyable little mid-Georgian house in Fore Street, with a Venetian window (24). But the most imposing brick front in Totnes is that of the former King Edward VI Grammar School, built in 1795. The building is otherwise all rubblestone. The doorway has an attractive fanlight, and there is another identical one inside. But until recently the brickwork was almost entirely obscured by a venerable mantle of ivy (25). Happily in November 1983 this was at last removed; but at the time of writing (early 1984) the building still awaits cleaning and repointing. It should then again become what it was when it was first erected: a handsome ornament to the town.

25. The old Grammar School (before the removal of the ivy in 1983)

Life in Georgian Totnes was genteel and pleasantly unhurried. Visitors all stayed at the Royal Seven Stars (28), which had been built about 1680, with mullioned and transomed windows and without, of course, the present quaint but top-heavy porch, which is early Victorian. But until about 1800 the roads were still very bad and most travellers came on horseback. When at last the condition of the roads improved, the coaches arrived.

About 1830 the 11th Duke of Somerset, the landowner, built another hotel, the Seymour (27), as a rival to the Seven Stars. This is in the suburb of Bridgetown, across the Dart, which was brought within the borough in 1834. Soon after this came a couple of handsome formal terraces, quite unlike anything to be found at Totnes before, or indeed since (26). A good many other houses, especially in the High Street, were refronted about this time, in a search for more architectural dignity and repose.

The South Devon Railway (broad gauge), built by Brunel, was opened from Exeter to Teignmouth in May 1846; to Newton Abbot that December; to Totnes in July 1847;

and on to Plymouth in 1849. This scenically beautiful line, which at Dawlish, hugging the coast, plunges through the same red Permian sandstone as had been used long before for the tower of Totnes church, originally employed the so-called atmospheric system of traction instead of the usual steam engines. Although the large iron air pipe was laid

26. *Devon Place*

27. *Seymour Hotel (closed 1983)*

*28. Royal
Seven Stars Hotel*

between the rails nearly as far as Totnes the system never operated beyond Newton Abbot, and in September 1848 had to be abandoned.[1] To many towns railways brought new industry, wealth and, all too often, ugliness. To Totnes it brought none of these. It led to the disappearance of the town's centuries-old river traffic without providing any fresh trade in its place.

So, during the second half of the nineteenth century the population fell from 3828 to 3116, and, apart from a couple of terraces near the station, hardly a single house was built here between about 1840 and 1914, for none was needed. Aesthetically, this was a great piece of good fortune for Totnes.

In recent years, however, prosperity has returned: three new industries have arrived, and all appear to be flourishing. A new Civic Hall was erected about 1960, with space for a market below (29). Some of the housing of the last generation is admittedly

[1]The failure was due to various causes, though the story that rats developed a taste for the grease on the leather pipe-valves and even for the leather itself has not been corroborated. The salt sea air presented a problem; and so did the difficulties of co-ordination between the pumping stations in pre-telegraph days.

unworthy, but some is notably good. I would single out two quite dissimilar buildings by the same hand: an older cider warehouse cleverly converted into a residence for elderly retired people, and, on the important river-bank site adjoining the Seymour Hotel, a block of flats interesting for its design and exactly right in scale. This is precisely the sort of place where nowadays some greedy developer, and an architect in league with him, will plead for a high-rise block – and sometimes, heaven knows how, get away with it, and ruin the town. But not here. To build today in an old town without spoiling it is neither easy nor, alas, common, so the architect should be named: he is R. G. Creber.

29.
The Civic Hall

In 1969 the whole of the old part of Totnes, some seventy acres in all, was, quite rightly, designated as a Conservation Area. An admirable Conservation Study was prepared by the Devon County Council, working in conjunction with the Town. Some of the recommendations have been carried out.

I would not claim that Totnes (which at the last census had 5627 inhabitants) is one of the most beautiful of our small towns. But it is certainly one of the most distinctive. And the preservation of that individuality is vital.